The Making of Airplane!

A Leaflet

JIM CRYNS

Copyright © 2019 by Jim Cryns

All rights reserved. No part of this book may be used or reproduced by any means, graphic, electronic, or mechanical, including photocopying, recording, taping, or by any information storage retrieval system, without the written permission of the publisher except in the case of brief quotations embodied in critical articles and reviews.

The intent of the author is only to offer general information to help you in your quest for emotional and spiritual welfare. In the event you use any of the information in this book for yourself or others, the author and the publisher assume no responsibility for your actions.

Table of Contents

Ready for Boarding Introduction 1

Kentucky Fried Theater 7

Kentucky Fried Movie 12

The Script 15

Howard Koch: The Producer 18

Directing Cubed 22

The Players 26

Robert Hays 29

David Leisure 33

Leslie Nielsen 37

Kareem Abdul-Jabbar 42

Jonathan Banks 48

Jill Whelan 51

Julie Hagerty 54

Lorna Patterson 58

Lee Bryant 62

Donna Pescow 64

Francesa 'The Kitten' Nativdad 66

Sandra Lee Gimple 67

Stephen Stucker	70
Shooting The Film	74
Jive Talkin'	83
Sequel? Fuhgeddaboudit	86
Who Cares What They Think?	87
Happy Landings	90

Ready for Boarding
Introduction

"I want the kids in bed by nine, the dog fed, the yard watered, and the gate locked. And get a note to the milkman... no more cheese!"

Surely you remember *Airplane!* The film with enough side-splitting quotes to fill a colloquial dictionary or a vaudeville trunk full of comedic bits. It's a comedy in the great realm of high school skits, Mad TV, In Living Color and the dog-eared screenplays people's nephews write in lieu of earning their college diplomas. It is sophomoric, obvious, predictable, corny, and always very funny. And the reason it's hilarious is frequently because it's sophomoric, predictable, corny. Yet, while the Zucker brothers and Jim Abrahams perfected their film parody technique by shooting basement versions of their favorite films and TV series, their comic sensibilities are pure Mad Magazine. "The movie parodies in Mad really pointed the way for us," said

David Zucker, whose bright-eyed Midwestern countenance belies his delight in humiliating cultural icons. "Scenes We'd Like to See and the movie parodies were our favorite. Even the stuff in the margins of Mad Magazine influenced what's happening on the periphery of our films.[1]" While watching *Airplane!*, subtitles are not required, just the same silly comedic mindset of David Zucker, Jerry Zucker and childhood friend Jim Abrahams (ZAZ). The stuff comes so fast a repeated viewing is almost always necessary to catch all the nuanced jokes. If you're *not* paying attention you're going to miss something. It's extremely difficult to make a deeply silly movie.

When people outside of Wisconsin think of the state, they might conjure images of Jeffrey Dahmer and Ed Gein, the guy Psycho was modeled after--two of our most famous or infamous exports. Perhaps a wheel of cheese, rolling pastures dotted with black and white cows would spring to mind. In a comedic vein it could be ZAZ, three Shorewood natives. Then again, maybe not. Wisconsin isn't known as an inherently funny

---

[1] Kent Black, New York Times, June 23, 1991

place but it has its moments. Forty years ago it was perhaps even less humorous than today. It was a 'flyover' state, synonymous with "Laverne and Shirley," bratwurst and beer. During the late fall and winter months in Wisconsin, humor doesn't grow on trees--nothing does.

In its first two days ZAZ's second feature film *Airplane!* released in 1980 grossed its entire $3.5 million dollar budget and by week's end it was comfortably in the black and ended up at about $85 million dollars. That's in 1980 money, making it the fourth largest grossing movie. That would be more than $250 million today. Not bad business for a film *nobody* wanted to make, labeling it sophomoric and juvenile. It's especially shocking when it came from three Hollywood nobodies, kids from Wisconsin no less. *Airplane!* captured a certain time and place in American history. Not only because of its reputation as one of the funniest films of all time, which it is, but the way it has worked itself into our lexicon and daily verbiage. How does a film do that? You or someone you know recites a line from the movie just about every day, even if it's subliminal. It just pops out of your mouth. You don't even plan to say them. There were so many great lines, if you didn't find one of them funny, there was no need to worry, another was already on its way.

"Joey, have you ever been in a Turkish prison?"

"Surely you can't be serious.' "I am serious...and don't call me Shirley."

"Looks like I picked the wrong week to quit sniffing glue."

"'S'mofo butter layin' me to da' bone. Jackin' me up...tight me!

In my personal vernacular *"What a pisser"* tends to come up a lot.

The list of quotation gems goes on and on. *Airplane!* had been rejected over and over, so it was rewritten many times, and that's subsequently why it was so tight. The jokes were silly and the humor flashed past the grasp of some of the studio executives who rejected it. Many of the actors didn't know what the hell to make of it either. You can't blame the executives or actors, this was off-the-wall stuff, a foreign language to them.

To distill this leaflet down to its essence, it's the story of three young guys from Shorewood who moved to Los Angeles and made a fortune in the film business. Sound reasonable? Not at all. If you'd written their story in a fictitious script a producer would have told you it was too far-fetched to be true, too fantastical to be believable. I spoke to both Zucker brothers, Jim Abrahams, Leslie Nielsen's daughter and every core cast member still living. This effort began as a book but ZAZ pulled out, and a leaflet was born.

Despite getting screwed over, I still respect and appreciate ZAZ. They've always known what they wanted. Somehow it was cemented in their minds early on, solely their vision and they pulled it off, despite all the naysayers. Yes, they had some comedy experience with their Kentucky Fried Theater, which we'll look at later. Those experiences spawned *Kentucky Fried Movie,* but *Airplane!* this was the big time. They were given a real budget, real actors and full sets, craft services, veteran producer.

What was the movie climate during the production on the film? There were a few films in the pipeline while *Airplane!* was being shot. Jerry Zucker said he doesn't think anyone around his film really knew anything about *Caddyshack*, "We were busy just getting through the days as best we could, knocking down challenges and making magic." Interestingly, people religiously quote *Caddyshack* almost as much as *Airplane!* The advent of the DVD around 1995 is largely responsible for both film's continued draw and viewing today.

Caddyshack also debuted in 1980, just three weeks after *Airplane!*. Both films have shared incredible longevity, zealous followings and widespread appeal. The dialogue and gags in *Airplane!* are a bit more rapid-fire and the story in *Caddyshack*, such as it is, tends to be marginally more in line with the traditional three-act-structure. *Airplane!* continued to gross twice as much as Caddyshack through the years, despite formidable firepower offered by Chevy Chase and Bill Murray. Surley, it was a force to be reckoned with--and I didn't call it Shirley.

Kentucky Fried Theater

"I had to ask the guy next to me to pinch me to make sure I wasn't dreaming."

ZAZ is comprised of three wisecracking kids in a suburb north of Milwaukee. They began honing their own brand of comedy anywhere they could--around the house, at neighborhood functions and then the library at the University of Wisconsin in Madison. When school became tedious, as is often the case for creative kooks, ZAZ concocted their own reality, looking for an outlet they gave birth to their own voice in comedy the only way they knew how.

In one scenario of their on-campus improv theatrics, some might say shenanigans, David would be pretending to study in the university library. When he took a break from the books in the library, he opened his briefcase, took out plates, candles, silverware, everything you'd need for an elegant dinner party--a virtual Downton Abbey. David would even light the candles for optimum effect as the rest of the bemused student body watched, wondering what the hell was going on. Abrahams would stroll into the library dressed as a waiter, complete with apron and bow tie. He laid a silver platter in front of David, who then lifted the lid to reveal a solitary McDonald's hamburger. David would proceeded to eat it as daintily as though he were Lady Mary Crawley. Odd humor? Hell yeah, but unarguably original; a creative outlet for ZAZ and a stress reliever for their unsuspecting, studious audience.

ZAZ's ideas are not so highfalutin. It's more like: So you think it'll get a laugh if her purse is full of sardines? Great, let's get some sardines in here.[2]

With roots in the often frozen ground of Wisconsin, a place better known for the Green Bay Packers and deer hunting than comedy troupes, the trio started The Kentucky Fried Theater in Madison. At first it was kind of a lark, but as time went on they began to take it more seriously. The creative energy had to come out somewhere, that's just the nature of

---

[2] Kent Black, New York Times, June 23, 1991

things. Kentucky Fried Theater was a bit of Second City, but more scripted and without the improvisation. The shows were well received by hip audiencess, many probably stoned out of their gourd, products of the late 60s and early 70s. The shows were well attended but ultimately weren't generating enough money to support the trio in Madison. Like a dog with a homeless guy who figures he can walk around on his own, the young men figured if they were going to starve, it'd be more pleasant to starve in Southern California. (New York was too hot in the summer and too cold in the winter.) After all, that's where everybody goes to pursue their dreams, isn't it? L.A.? It's near Hollywood, right?

They grabbed everything they had in Madison, not much of a task as there wasn't a whole lot, and stowed it in a U-Haul. This included chairs from the studio, plywood tables, everything they figured could be of some use in a potential theater in California. David said his parent's gave him and Jerry $3,000 a piece in cash and waved from their driveway, but nobody was exceedingly emotional at that moment. David said his parents figured they'd see them again real soon. "They'll be back," his parents assured each other. "After all, it is show business, right?"

As things were wrapping up at Kentucky Fried Theater, but before they left, they hosted a final show which captured the essence of the entire creative mission. On the opposite side of the back wall to the theater was a doughnut factory. They'd begin making delicious fresh doughnuts every night as the guys started performing. You could actually *smell* them baking in the kitchen. As usual, they were predictably unpredictable and ended up throwing doughnuts at the audience. Students in the audience would get higher than a kite, then go over and buy a bunch of doughnuts so they'd have something to eat during the show. That final night, Jerry got a big tray of doughnuts and lobbed them into the crowd. The audience loved it. They ate it up, literally speaking. They chowed down and then they even threw some back at the stage--reminiscent of a Madison version of the *Animal House* food fight.

Years later ZAZ discovered NBC producer Lorne Michaels had visited their live show in 1974 and said: "I want to do *that* on live network TV." The result was "Saturday Night Live", an instant hit and now the longest-running comedy in TV history.

Once in Los Angeles ZAZ opened up a storefront theater on Pico Boulevard, just down the street from the 20th Century Fox studios. This is where the Los Angeles' version of The Kentucky Fried Theater was birthed. After struggling to fill the theater with more than just a few people for each performance, they had a brainchild--they decided to rent the billboard on top of their building. Then they got all the friends and family they could to show up, creating a ruckus. They divided them into two groups telling one group 'you are protesting against this billboard eyesore and the other group ostensibly 'wanted to protect this historic landmark'. Then they did what any PR person worth their salt would advise--they called the local television station and got them to send out a remote unit to cover this 'breaking event.' In large letters on the billboard was the name of their 'long running' show, "The Nose." It was just a title, didn't mean anything except for the fact that when the reporter was interviewing all the protesters, the object of their concern was always in the background. It read, 'My Nose Runs Continuously.' The PR stunt worked. From that day forward, the theater was sold out.

Kentucky Fried Movie

"Ok give me Hamm on five and hold the Mayo."

After surprising success with the theater, thanks to their 'long running nose,' they were able to scrape up enough money to fund *Kentucky Fried Movie* in 1977, with neophyte John Landis directing. This was still two years before *Airplane!* It's crude, nude and not for the prude. As one of the first satire films ever made, this movie marks the historic birth of a subgenre that with time has come to generate a whole ocean's worth of offsprings. Very raunchy and experimental by form, yet for the better part quite funny. Some of the jokes are really top-of-the-line, even if the editing and visuals look awfully dated and low-budget. When they do hit their target, they hit hard. If you're easily offended by raw and unapologetic humor, you might want to take a pass because if there's one *Kentucky Fried Movie* as it doesn't hold back its punches.

Kentucky Fried Movie is a satirical anthology, a collection of shorter stories wrapped around a mini-film, directed by Landis, who later directed *Animal House, Twilight Zone*. *Kentucky Fried Movie* included cameos by Donald Sutherland, Bill Bixby, Henry Gibson, Tony Dow and many others. Admittedly some of the scenes in the film could make a grown man blush. However, with maturity comes discretion. Or at the very least, you acquire a sense of what you maybe would have thought about twice if given the chance. With regards to *Kentucky Fried Movie*, David Zucker said he still cringes at some of the sex depicted in the film. In the scene where the television news anchor observes the couple having sex on the couch, Zucker said he and his co-writers pretty much let the actors 'go for it.' The same scene was performed onstage at the Kentucky Fried Theater in Madison where it was received extremely well. ZAZ wanted to do was yank people out of their houses and if it took an R rated movie to do that, well, so be it.

ZAZ was looking for inspiration from all sources, including television. "For material, we'd leave the VCR on all night and see what turned up, check for commercials to parody," Jerry Zucker said. "One morning an actual movie caught our attention. It was called *Zero Hour!* So we purchased an option on the rights."

Airplane! is largely a classic because of a tight script based on the 1950s film, *Zero Hour!* ZAZ were watching late night television in Madison and *Zero Hour!* came on the tube. It was a decent film played deeply serious. At the same time they understood how it could be funny and they started riffing on the dialogue. *Zero Hour!* (yes, they even stole the exclamation mark) was a 1957 potboiler written by *Airport's* Arthur Hailey, and the trio swiped its absurd food-poisoning-at-30,000ft plot – and a lot of its dialogue – then besieged it with their full comedic powers. [3]

They knew they could build off of the script. You'd be floored if you knew just how many lines were taken verbatim from that film. ZAZ purchased the rights to *Zero Hour!* for a few thousand dollars.

---

[3] John Patterson, The Guardian, 2010

The Script

"You can tell me, I'm a doctor."

Zero Hour! was the spine of the movie and ZAZ fleshed it out, milked the funny and paid homage to the darkly serious. David Zucker said once a joke is made you don't let it hang around. For instance, the suicides in *Airplane!* Once a person self-immolated himself or hung himself above his seat, you never saw them again. You didn't see the crew scraping up the ashes or carrying the corpse to the back of the plane.

There is a ton of that kind of humor in Seth MacFarlane's 'Family Guy.' You cleared the decks for a new joke, got the debris out off the set, Peter Griffin has his arm back after it was severed in the last scene. A gag in *The Naked Gun* hit the audience, then disappeared. For example, when Lt. Drebin and Detective Ed Hokin are eating pistachio nuts that have been dyed red. They're eating a ton of nuts, tossing the shells out their respective windows. In the process, their lips and faces get smeared in red dye. But in the next scene, when Drebin is in Ludwig's office, he must be clean, there's absolutely no dye on his face. This wasn't a continuity error, that gag was ancient history, or it was like it never happened.

When the *Airplane!* script was being read by potential actors, they didn't know what to think, it was foreign to them. The rapid fire pacing you see in *Airplane!* was developed through their live theatre show, hundreds of live performances. Jokes in *Airplane!* come so thick and fast in their movies and they're delivered with such deadpan sincerity, it catches you by surprise. "We weren't really actors," Jerry Zucker said. "Just performers, so we were cheaper. We didn't even have the ability to make characters. All we could do was write jokes and act them out. We literally couldn't stand being on stage and not getting a laugh. A lot of people said their jaws ached after the show – and we wanted to get that on to film."

ZAZ are unselfish guys, so don't ask them who wrote what gag. They don't really recall and it just doesn't matter to them. One of the keys to a successful collaboration is to have minimal ego. They were never about taking credit. ZAZ worked toward a common goal--turning your insides out with laughter.

Pat Proft, who wrote the highly successful *Police Academy* movies and *Hot Shots,* partnered with ZAZ on the *The Naked Gun* films. He said somebody would bring an idea in and they'd just riff off that, all in the same room."We were on the same page right away. It felt like I was doing stuff back in Minnesota, it all came very easily," Proft told me during a phone conversation. ZAZ was brought up on similar comedy fuel, like Laurel and Hardy, Abbott and Costello. "We'd sit in a conference room and throw stuff out there, pick apart some genre films," Proft said. They drew from the kinds of things they liked, doing takeoffs and satires, throwing a lot of stuff against the walls. Sometimes it stuck, sometimes it fell to the ground in a tangled mess.

Howard Koch: The Producer

"You can't take a guess for another two hours?"

Airplane! producer Howard Koch had been an assistant director and had come up through the ranks, a real nuts and bolts kind of dude, not a guy to fuck with. He was a deal maker, knee breaker, and knew about getting important things like a bond for the film. He knew what you needed for this, how much you should pay for that. Koch knew all of the stuff ZAZ didn't know. He could make a call to Ethel Merman and get her to do a small part--and he did. Her last film role. Koch could do just about anything. He began his film career as an employee at the Universal Studios office in New York; then made his Hollywood filmmaking debut in 1947 as an assistant director. He worked as a producer for the first time in 1953 and a year later made his directing debut. Koch directed Mickey Rooney in *Andy Hardy Comes Home,* and *The Untouchables* with future *Airplane!* actor Robert Stack, among dozens of other projects. In 1964, Paramount

Pictures appointed him head of film production, a position he held until 1966 when he left to set up his own production company. By his own admission, Koch told 'The Guardian,' "There is not much I haven't done in the motion picture industry." It was Koch's participation that prompted Michael Eisner decide to sign off on a $3.5 million dollar budget for *Airplane!* If it weren't for Koch, the deal would not have been made, he was truly the man behind the curtain, the head honcho, the big cheese. Nobody would have taken the risk if Koch weren't involved, the the guy with experience, respect and a long history of success. By all accounts he was a cool, smooth guy. He had this way of walking that was really hip," David Zucker said. Koch worked with Frank Sinatra and produced several of his films including *The Manchurian Candidate, Sergeants Three, None but the Brave.* David Zucker said Sinatra was tough to deal with but if anybody could, it was Howard.

Actor Robert Hays, who played pilot Ted Striker, recalled walking into Koch's office, which he said had a huge heavy oak door with brass over it, looked expensive.. Hays said Koch was very hands-on as a producer. "You've got several types of producers," Hays said. "There are some that are just money people. They could be a rich dentist or doctor, maybe a Wall Street financier or someone who won the lottery. They're all terrific, but not necessarily 'film' people. Then there are people who knew film, like Koch, who handle the day-to-day stuff."

Hays said in the movie business everybody has to be on top of their game, that means directors, line producer, unit production managers, actors, the whole production. "If anyone is lagging, dragging their heels, it slows down the director," Hays said. "If a director is disorganized, that can create a whole new set of problems." Hays said ZAZ were excellent directors. Not only were they very well organized, they had Koch overseeing the whole deal, including the newbie directors. He was a father figure with a huge array of experience. He had been the head of Paramount and when he left as head of production, he'd negotiated a deal to have his production company, Howard Koch Productions, right there on the lot.

For the most part, ZAZ got to do *Airplane!* the way they wanted, the way they saw it in their heads. With

Koch at the helm, Paramount felt somewhat secure. It was their comedy and they insisted on directing, with the intense belief nobody else would 'get' what they were trying to do. When Michael Eisner at Paramount let the them do it *their* way, that was a very smart move on his part, and he was rewarded for it--mostly in cash. Then he allowed them to cast it the way they did. ZAZ knew from the onset they wouldn't have comic actors chewing up the scenery, like the Three Stooges or Marx Brothers. A comedic actor would have destroyed the gags and they weren't willing to cast one. The comedy is allowed to shine through when the absurd lines are delivered straight. Their vision broke the mold of comedy films.

Directing Cubed

"At this point, the entire digestive system collapses accompanied by uncontrollable flatulence."

ZAZ were a trio of newbies and really didn't know what the hell they were doing as directors, but they had a shot and weren't going to miss it. You never knew when it was going to come again.

During the *Airplane!* shoot, ZAZ had a small trailer on the set with a monitor where they'd watch specific scenes from *Zero Hour!* they had scheduled to shoot that day. "It was a refresher course, a blueprint, so to speak, on the nuances of the film that they could apply to our new movie," Jerry Zucker said. "I imagine part of that was for continuity of the story, to keep with the rhythm, as well as provide some kind of last minute inspiration." ZAZ, along with director of photography Joseph Biroc, captured the very angles used in *Zero Hour!* They were very melodramatic, which is great when you're making a film based on a film. It gave the movie a foreboding sense of tension. That heightened the comedy that quite often came out of left field anyway. This ties directly into their vision of using serious actors in comedic roles.

Julie Hagerty, who played the bemused stewardess Elaine Dickinson, said having more than one director was the norm, for all she knew. After all, this was her first movie. "Jerry was the one I dealt with most, he talked to the actors. Then after a scene they'd all congregate and talk. You'd hear this murmuring and Jerry would come over and say, 'Let's try this.' There was never any ad-libbing. They wrote the script and knew what they wanted. I watched the movie for the first time with ZAZ and Hays. Even they were laughing during the screening. I just go back and watch it every so often. It's so funny. It broke so much new ground."

Actress Lorna Patterson, who played the husband-less stewardess Randy, said ZAZ were always very precise about what they wanted. "It was about rhythms and how they wanted the jokes played," Patterson said. "One of the things that separates the truly inspired from everybody else is ZAZ knew with certainty who they were and what they could do. They didn't let anybody undermine that, even if nobody had attempted the same thing before." They had nothing to prove and abundant confidence in their abilities. "They basically made a movie that made them laugh and didn't pander," Patterson explained. "Then they had a champion in producer Howard Koch. With that combination, they couldn't lose."

It was Jerry Zucker who took on the role of the director talking with the actors, standing beside the camera. He was good at directing and later directed *Top Secret and Ghost.* After a given shot, the three would pow-wow to determine if they got what they wanted. Sometimes all three would come over to an actor and talk about a scene. The cast observed the striking thing about ZAZ was how well they knew each other. (Granted, two are brothers and one a childhood friend, but just the same.) One would start a sentence, another filled the middle and the third would finish it. That's how tight they were. None of them were competing to be top dog, like a lot of comedic personalities. They just knew what they were doing, trusted each other. Michael Eisner was also headstrong and knew what *he* wanted to see on the screen. ZAZ wanted to shoot the film in black and white and use an old prop plane, like *Zero Hour!*. Eisner disagreed and insisted the movie shot in color and for it to take place on a jet airliner, not an antiquated propellor plane. Once again ZAZ insisted. Eisner told them both were great ideas for making a movie, they just wouldn't be making *that* movie at Paramount. That conversation took place on a Friday. Eisner told them to take the weekend to figure out what really mattered to them. On Monday, ZAZ returned to Eisner's office and agreed to do it his way. ZAZ did get a zinger in on Eisner when they used the sound effects of a prop plane under the depiction of a jet airliner. That also ended up being a memorable joke in the film. It was not just funny, it also lent an ambience to the film--- a melodramatic drone that helped set the tone for the tension on the flight.

The Players

"Looks like I picked the wrong week to quit drinking."

The late rock jawed actor Peter Graves threw the script to the ground.'What kind of crap *is* this? What the hell *is* this crap?" His agent said, 'Look, this thing has got a lot of buzz going on about it. They say it's gonna be very funny and really good. You ought to look at it again.' So, Graves looked at it again and once again screamed, "I just don't get this crap! What the hell *is* this?" Still, his agent persisted, 'Look, just go on in and meet with the Zuckers.' So Graves met with ZAZ and he said, 'Well, I don't know. Maybe. It looks like it might be kind of funny. They seem like pretty funny guys." The next thing you know, there he is in the role of Captain Oveur, absolutely perfect for the role. The stoic actor known for *Stalag 17, Mission Impossible, The Night of the Hunter,* went on to play Captain Oveur in *Airplane II: The Sequel.*

ZAZ really trusted what their actors were doing. Actors say ZAZ were extremely comfortable to work with. Hays said he recalled one time they talked after a take. Jerry Zucker saw something was right with Hays. Jerry asked what the problem was. Hays squirmed a bit, trying to figure out how to tell them he was not totally happy with the take. "What is it, Bob? Do you want another take?" Jerry Zucker asked him. This was Hay's first feature film and he didn't want a reputation as a pain in the ass. He didn't want to be one of those actors that acts like a prima donna, costing them time and money. Jerry Zucker decided to do another take. Afterward he came up to Hays and said, "You were right, that was better!" Hays said it felt great, part of learning how each other worked. That friendship has endured for more than 40 years and Hays appears around the country at events with and for the Zucker brothers.

"My agent, Arnie Soloway, was known to his clients as the 'hustler with a heart'," Hays explained. "He was very good at negotiating deals. He knew television better than he knew films and was pretty old school, had a sense of the old style. Like some of my fellow actors early on, I didn't really have a sense of building my career." Hays spent a lot of his time going out on interviews and taking what he could get to build a resume. It was mostly television, (although he did go in, along with a million other guys, to read for the part of Hans Solo in a Sci-Fi western like thing called *Stars Wars*. Rumor has it the movie did quite well. Needless to say Hays didn't get it.

His agent took him on his daily rounds to meet the casting directors. It was great for Hays. Instead of them just having a headshot to look at, they got to meet him and get a sense his personality. It helped a lot. Hays managed to land over two dozen roles in about a year and a half, working in small one and two line parts, up to guest star shots. Then came his big break as Brad on the television show 'Angie', a mid-season replacement on ABC, starring Donna Pescow (from *Saturday Night Fever*) in the title role. Hays was her unbelievably wealthy new husband, who had not followed his father into the family international conglomerate business. Instead Brad decided to become a pediatrician instead----still full of money. It was during 'Angie' when Hays auditioned for and got the role of Ted Striker in *Airplane!*

Robert Hays

a.k.a. Ted Striker

"I know. I know. But it's his ship now, his command; he's in charge, he's the boss, the head man, the top dog, the big cheese, the head honcho, number one."

Jerry Zucker remembers when he was first made aware of Hays. "Howard Koch brought in Bob's photo-on-resume, the typical 8 x 10 thing and he plunked it down. He said, 'Hey, what do you think about this guy?' I mean, Howard didn't particularly know him. I don't even know if he'd seen "Angie." But at that point, we just hadn't found anyone to play Ted, so it was, like, 'Sure, he looks nice. Bring him in.' But I don't think Bob was ever, like, the great hope. Like, 'God, this guy could really be it.' He was just Tuesday at 10 o'clock. But then Bob came in, and it was like, 'Thank God!'"

The first time Hays read the script for *Airplane!* he was on a flight to Minneapolis. Hays played Lt. Ted Striker, the fighter pilot with a 'drinking problem.'

Hays said there was something on every page that made him laugh out loud. "There was a stewardess, very prim and proper, bun in her hair, who saw him laughing and asked what I was reading," Hays said. "I told her it was a script for a film I was up for and asked her if she wanted to read it. She said sure. So, she sat down and started to read it and pretty soon her hair was undone and she was all over the place, laughing hysterically."

Hays is a Marine brat who started out at the Old Globe Theater in San Diego and went on to star in over 20 feature films and got to be a presenter at the Academy Awards–twice. He also hosted 'Saturday Night Live' during their lean years. He said he won the lottery when he won the part of Striker, feeling as though he'd awoken from a wonderful dream. Each day he could hardly contain his enthusiasm to rush to the set. He grew to realize it was more than just a dream, that it actually happened.

Hagerty knew Hays from his ABC show "Angie," "One time he brought Donna Pescow over from the 'Angie' studio to see how things were going on *Airplane!*," Hagerty said. "It was always so nice to be around him, a non-competitive environment. He was always running back and forth between our set and the one on 'Angie.' It overlapped for at least a couple of weeks. I imagine it was pretty hectic for him but he never brought any of that stress or emotional luggage to our set. He'd show up, disappear, show up, disappear. Robert is what he is, nothing negative about him."

"Have you ever woken from a dream feeling so good because you'd dreamed you had just won the lottery?" Hays asked me. "Well, I do that now and again. I wake up from a wonderful dream that I had auditioned for a feature--my first--and had gotten the part. Not just a part, but the lead in a comedy that was so fun to make it probably is illegal in some states--certainly in some countries! Everyday you couldn't wait to get to the set." And then, on becoming fully awake, instead of realizing it was just a dream, I get to realize that it wasn't. It actually happened."

Hays said he's an actor who reacts to other actors. "In *Airplane!* I think Ted and Elaine were the only *sane* ones in the bunch. All the insanity seemed to revolve around us. Even though we all played it straight, I figured I was always the character people could relate to, from the audience's point of view. In the scene when Dr. Rumack and Randy are in the cockpit with Ted, and they repeat Ted's line, "It's a entirely different kind of flying--altogether," I apparently raised my eyebrow in reaction. I didn't think about it at the time, it was just natural. But ZAZ came in after seeing it in the dailies and told me they hadn't seen it when they were shooting, but saw it up on the big screen. They came running in saying, 'You lifted your eyebrow and it was great. That was funny!' ZAZ were really appreciative of what all actors brought to their roles. Everyone was so honest and pure in their interpretation of their characters."

"If you look at a blooper reel on "Angie," you'll see he does this little Popeye whisper into my ear," "Angie" co-star Donna Pescow said. "At first I didn't know what was going on but he did. I just broke down in laughter and he'd act like he had no idea what was happening, just look at the director and shrug. He knew just what button to push and I fell for it every time. We became such good friends."

David Leisure
a.k.a. Hare Krishna

"No thanks, we gave at the office."

David Leisure auditioned four times for the same Hare Krishna part. Four times for about a minute of screen time. Only in Hollywood. They had another actor that kind of looked like Leisure, almost like brothers, so they hired him too. They shaved Leisure's head on the first day on set and he had to keep it shaved for six weeks. All he had left was a little tail the Krishnas wear. When he put on the robes on set it was all pretty strange. When he was asked to shave his head he was worried he was going to look like Mr. Clean from the floor cleaner commercials. So, for six weeks he did indeed look like Mr. Clean. If Leisure wasn't wearing his baseball hat, you could hear people whispering and muttering, 'Hey, look at that guy over there.' "I didn't have an opinion about the Krishna movement one way or the other when I got the role," Leisure said. "But I will say that it was really hard to figure out how to put on what they wear, because it wraps around, and you have to pull it between your legs. Then you tuck it in."

When Leisure first read the script for *Airplane!* he admits he didn't get the 'joke,' like a ton of other people. "I thought, this just looks like words to me. I don't see what's so funny. And it wasn't until I realized they'd used all of these really, really serious guys and had them be really, really serious, which turned out to be funny. Then I finally got the joke. I'm a little slow."

Leisure had known Hays since 1968 when they were roommates in college. "He's my oldest and best friend," Leisure explained. "He has a tough as nails sister. His mom was like four feet tall on a box, kind and warm. Some of the greatest people I ever met. Bob's father was a Marine Colonel, so they moved to a lot of different places. He was exposed to a lot of the world and that may have had something to do with his being so friendly and outgoing." The first time Hays invited him out for a drink, Leisure said he was flattered. "I realized I was going to hang out with this chick magnet. I even started to dress like Bob--and it worked. He always wore a white long john shirt with a denim shirt over it with the sleeves rolled up and jeans." With a Van Dyke beard Leisure said Hays looked like Wild Bill Hickok. "Once we got to San Diego State, we majored in how well we could roll a joint or tap a keg. Our hearts were young and gay. A friend of mine said I should get in the drama department as it was easy. Acting was good for me, cathartic, and I developed a sense of humor as a defense mechanism. When I was young I was overweight. I also had an unsightly problem. I got hit in the head by a baseball bat and lost a front tooth. My parents were so cheap they had the dentist put in a stainless steel tooth. I was way ahead of the gangsta curve. So, I had to develop a sense of humor to deal with that."

"This was my first film gig and I was starstruck," Hays said. "I'm sitting in a chair looking at all these legends like Robert Stack, Lloyd Bridges, Peter Graves. I rarely saw Bob on the set as he was off doing a different scene. I didn't have any experience being on a movie set. What I do remember is ZAZ' efforts to make everyone feel comfortable, like they belonged. I have to say the coolest guy on the set was Howard

Koch, who took a paternal interest in the project and made it easy to be part of the production. He was there every day and made the film what it is."

Leisure and Hays go all the way back to Grossmont College, and then were roommates at San Diego State University. Hays remembers being up in the offices during casting and there were different people they were suggesting and saying, "These are potential folks." Hays pointed at Leisure and said, "Oh! He's a buddy of mine! We went to school together. He's a great guy!" Hays doesn't recall if ZAZ said, "Oh, okay, yeah, he's in. We'll use him," or if they'd chosen him already. He really can't remember. He just remember saying, "Oh, that's my buddy Dave." I found out he had already been in to read three times. Anyway, he was great. I don't know if it was before or after Airplane, but Dave went on to star as Joe Isuzu, the world's greatest liar, in what became some of the most famous commercials of all time."

Leslie Nielsen

a.k.a. Dr. Rumack

"Sometime, when the crew is up against it, and the breaks are beating the boys, tell them to get out there and give it all they got and win just one for the Zipper. I don't know where I'll be then, Doc," he said, "but I won't smell too good, that's for sure."

Thea Nielsen Disney knew her father had an interesting job, but never saw him have a better time than when he worked on *Airplane!* Nielsen Disney is an actress known for *Dracula: Dead and Loving It* (1995) *Wrongfully Accused* (1988) and *Family Plan* (1997).

"I got to see my father stoked to do a job, express love for his work," Nielsen Disney said. "He got to expand on that with the *The Naked Gun* series. He was born to play those parts. My father trusted me a lot and he asked me to read the script for *Airplane!* I remember being at his house reading the script and he and I were a lot alike. I told him it was amazing, like it was written *for* him. If you want to know my dad, just picture Frank Drebin singing the National Anthem or just about anything else Frank Drebin did."

Lee Bryant played a wife and mother who went hysterical later in the film and was methodically slapped by other passengers. She said she'd seen Nielsen in a lot of projects before *Airplane*! but this was different.

"He was always a very serious actor, played the heavy," Bryant said. "I ran into him in Hawaii and we had dinner a couple of times. I was with my daughter, he was with his. I was surprised at how vastly entertaining and funny he was at dinner. If any of the actors tried to be funny it would have telegraphed the comedy and never would have worked. The total success of the movie depended on that not happening. Everybody got along so well. We laughed and laughed. I remember David had enough of Leslie's fart makers, which he'd sold to everybody in the cast. He probably made more with those than his salary. David sent a basket around telling everybody to put their fart makers in to quiet the set."

Nielsen Disney once said it was the nature of the humor that drew her father to the project. "He said he was never trying to tell the audience what was funny and what wasn't," Nielsen Disney said. "He said he couldn't *show* or *telegraph* what the joke was. His job was to just put it out there. If you missed it, you'd have to see the movie a second time. In comedy, the moment the audience sees you know what the joke is, it's over. They're not going to laugh.

"My dad said he didn't really recognize how funny it all was until he saw *Airplane!* at a screening with a test audience," Nielsen Disney said. "Dad said audience members were clutching their sides they were laughing so hard. The moment the film came out, producer Howard Koch told him it would be a hit. From then on, Nielsen would be known for the line, 'Don't call me Shirley.'"

"When my father died he must have had some fan page in existence," Nielsen Disney said. "The outpouring of emotion I read from fans after his death blew my mind. Yes, I understand he was an actor, people paid to see his movies, but this was beyond that. Every once in a while I'll still see a comment online about him and it amazes me that he touched so many people. He was without ego, he just wanted to make people laugh. It was meant for him to do a comedy like *Airplane!* Sure, the money was lovely, but I know how much he adored the work, it fed him and made him who he was. I knew he was happy because he called and said he'd made chicken soup. He did that when he was happy. That was how I took my dad's 'temperature.' If he made soup, all things were good."

Nielsen Disney said it was never a big deal to see her father on a film--it was her life. It was like, 'Oh, Dad's in a movie.' She only knew it as his job. Nielsen Disney was just nineteen when the film came out and was thrilled her father was part of the project. He'd always been known as a broad range actor, but never associated with comedy. She thinks her father finally felt he was being seen for the guy he was. She knew the goofy guy. Finally, the world got to see him. "When I first saw the movie I was thinking, 'Oh, dad got a job,'" Nielsen Disney said. "But the more I watched, the more I thought it was so funny, hilarious. They were the first of a generation to offer that kind of comedy, really groundbreaking stuff. There were parodies before the movie but nothing this clever and it needed serious actors to pull it off."

"Around the house, there was no fart machine. We got the real thing. He was in his underwear a lot."

Nielsen Disney recalled her father's initial experiences with ZAZ. "It suddenly dawned on him he wasn't being cast against type. The fact was he was always cast against type before *Airplane!*." This was her father's chance to let go, do what he really wanted, be a crazy guy. Turn that guy loose. This was the key to Nielsen's freedom. When the smoke cleared, he found out he was still alive and got a license to be nuts. Even though he'd already made more than 50 movies and put in almost a thousand TV appearances, Leslie Nielsen knew ZAZ and Frank Drebin are what made him, at long, long last, a big fat star.[4]

---

[4] Tom Shales, The Washington Post, June 28, 1991

Kareem Abdul-Jabbar
a.k.a. Roger Murdoch

"Listen Kid! I've been hearing that crap ever since I was at UCLA. I'm out there busting my buns every night. Tell your old man to drag Walton and Lanier up and down the court for 48 minutes."

NBA Hall of Fame player Kareem Abdul-Jabbar was ecstatic to get the chance to work with Peter Graves. "I thought Peter Graves was a cool guy, very easy to work with," Abdul-Jabbar said. "He didn't have any movie star attitude. He taught me to approach acting as a professional, not as an athlete playing at acting. He taught me to be prepared, know my lines, know what I wanted to accomplish in the scene and stay focused."

Actors in the film have lines, familiar quotes from the film, tossed at them from fans around the world. It can be annoying after 30 years, but Abdul-Jabbar said you kind of get used to it. "Every few months someone will holler a line at me on the street and give me a thumbs up," Abdul-Jabbar said. "*Airplane!* came out in 1980 so I've been hearing people quote lines to me for 39 years. You'd think it would get old or annoying, but it really doesn't. It's gratifying to know that I was part of something that has been giving people pleasure for nearly four decades."

If you've met Abdul-Jabbar, you were probably struck by his introspection and few words. Jerry Zucker said he came up to Abdul-Jabbar's his belt buckle. "We immediately saw him as the gentle and intelligent man he was." In negotiations with Abdul-Jabbar his agent asked for $10,000 more than he was offered. "He wants to buy a rug," his agent told Zucker. "Not the kind you walk on, but an art piece." Zucker said that was the most ingenious agent ploy he'd ever heard and agreed to the pay increase. They assumed it was just a ploy, but a couple of weeks later they saw a picture of Abdul-Jabbar in "Time" magazine and there he was, standing in front of an ornate Oriental rug. Brilliant.

Actor David Leisure, who played the Hare Krishna guy on the plane, recalls Abdul-Jabbar was a kind and gracious man. "I walked on the set and saw him there," Leisure said. "This was right after the Lakers had won a championship. Abdul-Jabbar was the MVP of the series. As I've said, putting a man of that size in the cockpit was hilarious, a great gag. I was surprised to find out how shy he was. I didn't know about Pete Rose being the initial choice for that role, never heard about it. But they couldn't have done any better than Kareem."

Abdul-Jabbar said he understood the humor right away as a combination of parody and theater of the absurd. "They were using metafiction in the same way as Mel Brooks did in *Blazing Saddles*, using the conventions of the genre to blend the story with reality, Abdul-Jabbar said. "They used the public perception that I was prickly and to poke fun at me and that perception. The scene where Barbara Billingsley from "Leave It to Beaver" says she speaks jive was funny and topical."

Abdul-Jabbar said the first time he saw the film the studio had set up a screening for him in a theater. "I brought my kids. It was the first time I saw my face thirty feet tall and it was a bit of a shock for me and my kids. Something about the size detaches you from your own image, as if you're seeing yourself for the first time. Like traveling back in time and running into your younger self."

Each of the cast and crew have their favorite parts of the movie. "There's the scene where the flight attendant sings to a sick little girl and gets so into it she knocks the IV out of the girl's arm," Abdul-Jabbar said. "The flight attendant and the passengers are all rocking along with the song while the little girl is convulsing. And Peter Graves and I hear the singing and smile at each other. That makes me laugh." If you knew Abdul-Jabbar, you'd know it takes a lot to make him laugh.

Casting Abdul-Jabbar as co-pilot Roger Murdoch may have seemed crazy. But like the rest of the film, it came from *Zero Hour!*. That film cast football legend Elroy 'Crazylegs' Hirsch as Captain Bill Wilson, the pilot. Hirsch acquired the "Crazylegs" nickname because of his unusual running style in which his legs twisted as he ran. The part of Roger Murdoch was originally intended for baseball legend Pete Rose, but the deal couldn't be done as Rose was still busy with baseball. "Our working relationship was very straightforward," Abdul-Jabbar said. "The only thing they said to me about my role was, 'Everyone knows you're an incredible athlete. What if you applied the same ethics to another job?' So, I acted as I would have had I been a co-pilot instead of a basketball player, though in the movie I was actually both."

Abdul-Jabbar said he learned quickly. "When you first arrive and don't know your way around the set. Eventually you find the AD, (assistant director) or a PA, (production assistant). They are the ones who know where everything is and where you're supposed to be. Usually it's 'Toss your stuff in your trailer there and get in makeup and hair right now. You're up first.' They hustle you over to the makeup trailer and ask what you'd like from the caterer's wagon," Abdul-Jabbar said. "Then, as they apply your makeup, you sneak a bite of your breakfast whenever they turn to get something. After that, it's back to your trailer where the wardrobe department folks have set up your costume for whatever scene you're shooting that day. You are given 'sides' of the scenes and go over those to refresh your memory, or just relax a bit and gather yourself, or, as in my case, you start wandering over in the direction of the set to see what's going on."

Jonathan Banks

a.k.a. Radar Operator

"He's all over the place--900 feet up to 1,300 feet, what an asshole."

While Jonathan Banks has enjoyed a huge career with 'Breaking Bad' and 'Better Call Saul,' he only had a minor role in *Airplane!* as a radar man. "I had a really good time working with everyone," Banks said. "I went in, it was a job, but between the brothers and Jim Abrahams, it was all so good. It's been a long time so I'm still trying to piece some things together. I think a lot of the success of the movie comes because of the time it came out of. It's difficult to make a broad-stroke generalization of the social climate, but I think the movie was refreshing. Hollywood was riddled with a lot of negative stuff and this was a bit of fresh air." Banks has appeared in films through the years such as *48 Hours, Beverly Hills Cop, Mudbound* and *Incredibles 2*.

"There was such an absurdity in that film, such

constant fun," said Banks. "I turn it on and still laugh. Bob Hays and I didn't work at the same time together on *Airplane!* but we did later on a film titled or *Better or For Worse* in 1990. Bobby's a kind guy, a good friend. He knows I like beer and around Christmas time I always get a cool selection of different kinds of beer. How cool is that? I have a daughter who's 49-years-old. She 'gets' the film. I have 23-year-old twins and I don't know if they've discovered *Airplane!* I might have to tell them."

Hollywood can be a tight community. Hays had already been friends with Leisure for decades and working with Banks helped cultivate another solid friendship.

"I've seen another side of Bob," Banks said. "We were working in Spain and we were in this beautiful place on the Mediterranean, hitting the clubs, and we didn't have a ride home. So, we start to walk back toward the hotel, laughing, trying to hitchhike. Suddenly this guy in a car thinks he's funny, swerves toward us like he's going to hit us. Without missing a beat, Bobby kicks and got a good crack at the door. The car screeches to a halt in the gravel, smoking its wheels and the driver jumps out. He takes one look at Bobby, sees he is frothing at the mouth, hops back in his car and takes off. He's a great guy, unless you mess with him. We became great friends after that."

Jill Whelan

a.k.a. Little Sick Girl

"Oh Mother, isn't this exciting?"

Certainly you recall girl on the gurney in the front of the plane on her way to the Mayo Clinic. Jill Whelan, who played the 'sick little girl' attached to an IV in the movie, said Koch was one of the most amazing people she'd ever known. "I showed up for my first day on the set and soundstage, just in a whirlwind. I felt like Alice falling down the hole," Whelan said.

"We were standing in the small fuselage of the plane. I didn't know where to go or what to do. Then, through the lights and chairs comes Howard Koch. He puts his arm around my shoulder and starts walking with me and telling me everything I should know on a set." Along the way, Whelan said Koch said hello to the crew by name, asking how their kids were. "He sat me in a chair and gave me a lifelong lesson. He said if you're ever on a movie set and you hear a loud noise, an explosion, don't look up! Cover your head. He said it could be a light exploding and that could hurt you. I never forgot that. Years later, maybe on 'The Love Boat,' I heard a loud pop and then I heard Howard's voice in my head. I did exactly what he told me. I bent forward and covered my head and glass fell all over me. His words could have saved my face. He was just like a father."

"I think the reason *Airplane!* appeals to so many people is because it brings us together, we're all in on the joke," Whelan said. "It's like a community. When you're friends with someone you share things. This movie is a shared experience. For whatever reason we connect with it. It grounds us. This movie really broke the mold. We knew the movie was going to be a huge success or a huge failure. My mother and I chose to go to a regular theater instead of the Hollywood premiere. The audience just went crazy for it."

Whelan said she was a newbie in the business when she auditioned, probably 11 years-old. "I walked through these doors that must have been ten feet high and they were golden. I knew I was someplace different," Whelan said. "I did a simple read and he asked me to make a funny face. I gave him the best fish-lipped face I could muster and I got the job. Howard Koch was such a lovely man. I remember a couple of years after the movie my mom drove me to his house and I gave him some chocolate chip cookies. Aaron Spelling wanted to put me under contract but my attorney at the time said 'no.' He told me he didn't want me working anywhere else. I did an episode of "Love Boat" and it aired. Suddenly people were calling in, sending letters that they really liked the family aspect of Captain Stubing having a daughter on the ship. Then they wanted me back right away. I didn't have any fear or trepidation because I was so young. I wasn't seasoned enough to be nervous. I worked with so many interesting people on that show; Ethel Merman, Douglas Fairbanks Jr., Lillian Gish, Gene Kelly."

Julie Hagerty

a.k.a. Stewardess Elaine Dickinson

"Ladies and gentlemen, this is your stewardess speaking. We regret any inconvenience the sudden cabin movement might have caused. This is due to periodic air pockets we encountered. There's no reason to become alarmed and we hope you enjoy the rest of your flight. By the way, is there anyone on board who knows how to fly a plane?"

Hagerty said when she looks back on the movie, she recalls having fun with Hays. "I'm always reminded of how we did the movie from our hearts and we'd giggle and say to each other, 'here comes the funny stuff."

"The movie makes me laugh. I think the whole movie is about reacting. It comes from an honest place." Hagerty said she recalls when Randy the stewardess was saying goodbye to the passengers as they exit at the end, sliding down the inflated ramp. 'Goodbye, have a nice day," Randy told them. "That's very funny," Hagerty said. "Working with our childhood heroes was particularly fun. Barbara Billingsley was Beaver's mom. How fun is that? Suddenly, out of the blue, she's speaking jive." Hagerty said the role of Elaine Dickinson gave her a career. "It helped so many of us."

Producers have tried to make another movie like *Airplane!* They just can't do it. People think, 'I can make a movie like that,' but they are only taking a swing. They fail. All they can see is the money made on the first film. The original film was imbued with something special and it worked collectively. People had never seen anything like it before. That's why it endures. That's also why *Airplane II: The Sequel* was such a bomb.

"I'm always surprised when people come up and tell me how much they love it and I got to be in it," Hagerty said. "There was one naysayer. My Grandma Hagerty pulled me aside one day and asked, 'When are you going to make a nice movie?' You can't please everybody. I guess it was a little ahead of her time. I was there when they did the sweating sequence. It was important not to break character in a very funny scene.

There was one exception to that and it was Leslie. He always broke the scene with his fake flatulence. The studio executives would come over and ask what was happening. but it was Leslie so you could forgive him." You could *always* forgive Leslie.

Before she landed her role in *Airplane!*, pun intended, Hagerty was working off-off-off Broadway at her brother's theater. Michael Hagerty was a founder of the Production Co. an Off-Off Broadway group. "You have to remember when you're working in such a small theater you get maybe 60 people in the audience. Then I got the call to audition for *Airplane!* They had me do a good old fashioned screen test, like they did in old Hollywood. It was a screen test I did with Robert. It was nerve-wracking of course. Robert didn't seem nervous, his middle name should be 'easy.' Nothing seems to ruffle his feathers. The screen test was done in a very small room depicting a hospital with just a few chairs, a bed that Bob was in." They did the scene in the hospital where Ted is recovering from an emotional breakdown.

Hagerty said after the test she went back to New York and didn't hear anything for a couple of months, which is par for the course in the business. "You don't dwell on an audition. You either get it or you don't. Robert and I both got the parts and it was pretty cool to think I'd be going to L.A. to shoot a feature film."

Lorna Patterson

a.k.a. Randy the Stewardess

"Oh, Dr. Rumack, I'm scared. I've never been so scared. And besides, I'm 26 and I'm not married."

Lorna Patterson, who played Randy the stewardess, said they were on a tight budget and they only had two of the gag life preservers for the pre-takeoff instructions. "They used CO_2 cartridges to make the rubber expand and fill with air and the duck was to pop up fast," Patterson said. "In rehearsal, we blocked the scene and I pretended to pull the cord. I'd pantomime it. They strapped the cartridges to my shoulder and I was wearing a thin white blouse. When we shot the scene, I pulled the cord, the cartridges went off and they burned. It was ice cold. We did the shot and I tried to hold still, keep from screaming, but I was in great pain and couldn't continue the scene. They asked what the problem was and I told them it was burning, like I was on fire. For the last inflatable duck, they put a pad under the cartridges and we got it." Ah, the aches and pains actors endure for their craft.

Patterson said they were all very young and for many it was the first time on a movie set. The older and established actors create a safe environment. "We didn't really know what we were doing and were happy to be in a movie," Patterson said. "But it was fun, a really nice experience. I don't know that we had even a clue, an inkling of a clue how big this was going to be. I was a very young actress going on auditions, trying to get minimum paying jobs. I'm a teacher now and my kids seemed to find *Airplane!* between ages of ten and fourteen, regardless of the era they were born into. They always ask if I'll sing "River of Jordan" for their bar mitzvah. They quote the movie and it has become timeless. A lot of the lines from the film have become a part of our culture. We laugh to this day and it transports us to a simpler time."

Patterson had some great successes early in her career. She had a regular spot on "Working Stiffs" with Michael Keaton. Later she landed the role of Pvt. Judy Benjamin in the CBS television show "Private Benjamin" based on the eponymous film with Goldie Hawn. She worked alongside the great Eileen Brennan.

Patterson gave up screen acting in 1993. She's married to film director Michael Lembeck.

"I think Lorna was tremendous as Randy," David Zucker said. "She came in to read, she was very good looking and could sing. She really owned it. Lorna was a huge part of this movie, just hysterical. Her reactions were amazing and the scene with Leslie and her not being married is classic. I think she is a stronger comedic actress than people have given her credit for. She was so darling."

"I'd already been cast as Randy and ZAZ said there was a problem and asked my agent if I could sing," Patterson said. "I ran over to their office with a cassette tape in my hand from my voice lessons. I asked if they had a tape player in the office. I guess I just assumed they had one. All three of them were running around the office looking for one, sandwich wrappers and half-eaten lunches everywhere. It looked like a scene from a Marx Brothers movie. When they couldn't find a tape player, I told them I could sing acapella. Jerry said no, he had a tape player in his car." They ran out to the lot. Lorna jumped in the back seat, Jerry took the seat next to her. David and Jim hopped into the front seat of an old Volvo. "I put on the tape, turned around and sang," Patterson said. "It was just the four of us in the car. I always say I auditioned for *Airplane!* in the backseat of a Volvo."

"There was a ton of innocence. None of us were jaded. It was all-for-one and one-for-all on the set," Patterson said. "It kind of set me up in a bad way as I never had as good experience again on anything I worked on. Other jobs were full of egos and more like work. Not the playful feeling we had on this movie. *Airplane!* was a magical little moment in time where everything came together. I didn't see all the humor in the script, that's the absolute truth. Am I naturally funny? Yes. Did I do a little improvisation? Yes. When the passengers were sliding down the rubber ramp at the end of the movie, it was me that was cracking them up. You can see some of them laughing. Jerry came up and asked the extras why they were laughing? They said because I was cracking them up. I was telling them to "Have a nice day," and "Thanks for flying Trans-American."

Lee Bryant

a.k.a. Slapped Wife

"Jim never has a second cup of coffee at home."

"Nobody was getting rich as we were paid scale for the film," Lee Bryant said. Bryant played the wife of the guy who never has a second cup of coffee at home. "Nobody knew what we were doing and I couldn't make a lot of sense out of the script when I read it. Like a lot of people, it started to make sense after I watched it on the screen. One of the surreal parts of that bit was Bryant had appeared in the very Yuban coffee commercial ZAZ were parodying. They had no clue. "I didn't want to tell ZAZ that I'd done the Yuban commercial because I didn't want them to think they were typecasting the role. Nick Pryor is a wonderful actor and friend of Bryant's. "We worked on the SAG board together. I told him at the time, I knew why *I* was doing the film, I needed the credit. Then I asked him why *he* was. He told me he thought the movie would serve us both well in our careers, just had a feeling it would be a hit. Of course he was right."

In the film *Zero Hour!* they shook the woman up a tiny bit but I told ZAZ it'd be funny if they slapped me. They were worried I'd get hurt but I told them not to worry. We'd stage it. The whole bit would be funny. Sometimes they came close to hitting me. Leslie couldn't seem to get the timing right." Bryant jokes.

Donna Pescow

"Hey, you know what they say. See a broad, to get that booty yak 'em."

Donna Pescow recalls the dance shoot in the seedy bar. "Robert asked me to come by and see the shooting of the dance sequence," she said. "I stood in the back and thought I was going to blow the take because I was laughing so hard, it was hysterical. John Travolta was shooting *Urban Cowboy* on the lot and he and Hays had never met. John and I were good friends after we made *Saturday Night Fever* and I wanted them to meet. The assistant director on *Urban Cowboy* got us in and John came over and they got along famously. John asked about *Airplane!* and Robert felt awkward telling John they were shooting a spoof on the *Saturday Night Fever* dance scene," Pescow said. "Meanwhile, John is being called every few minutes to get back to work but he enjoyed hanging out with Bob. The amazing thing about Robert running between our set and the film set was he never shortchanged either side. He never asked the producers on "Angie" to lighten the load to make it easier on him. He didn't expect anybody to change anything for him. Oddly, people would have been happy to do it for him because he was so kind."

As far as the crazy dance sequenced is concerned, they had Hays in a harness and started moving him around, jerking him from side to side. They finally yanked him out of the scene. Then came the Kozachok (some say the Kozatski,) ZAZ's version of the Russian dance where you shoot out one leg and then the other. Pretty soon, Hays was shooting both legs out at the same time. People asked how he did that and he jokingly told them he really worked out a lot. "Some figured out I obviously had wires holding me up, which of course was true," Hays said. "As I was kicking out my legs, Jim Abrahams asked if I could juggle. I said yep and he tossed me a few oranges. Sometimes a gag is invented extemporaneously during shooting and that one worked well. You can see Julie in the background in her cute red dress and red bow in her hair standing with the extras cheering me on when I did the Russian dance, legs off the ground."

Francesa 'The Kitten' Nativdad
Shaking Boobs Lady

" Oh stewardess, I speak jive."

During the 'can anyone fly a plane?' sequence, most people will remember a woman flashing her prodigious breasts in panic. That was Francesa 'The Kitten' Nativdad. "I was originally cast to walk through security and they told me they had something else for me," she explained. "I'm a burlesque star so I had no problem getting naked. Jerry just told me to shake them up. I remember the crew talking about my boobs and all the cast was asking how I lived with breasts so large. But it was a great experience. For ads for *Airplane II,* they had me straddling an airplane and that got me into Playboy magazine."

Sandra Lee Gimple

Fighting Girl Scout

"I like my coffee like I like my men...Black!"

When was the last time you witnessed two Girl Scouts kicking the shit out of each other? Sandra Lee Gimple played one of the two Girl Scouts brawling in the Magumba bar. It was the first girl-on-girl fight in a movie--being Girl Scouts was icing on the cake. She was in the Magumba bar scene with Paula Marie Moody. She's the one who had her head slammed into the jukebox to start the Bee Gee's song, 'Staying Alive.' "The script was funny," Gimpel said. "They needed two stunt girls that could stage this fight and we were supposed to be young. To help with that they used Ace bandages to press down our boobs. Everybody loves this film. Kids still come up to me and say, 'I can't believe you were in that movie.' It feels good to be part of something so historic. This one is one of the few I've done that really stands out. It took a while to shoot the dance scene and we were on the set the whole time.

They kept us a week. They wanted me to fall down this big staircase. After *Airplane!* Jerry directed me on another film. In that one Jerry wanted this stunt person to look like a heavy Debbie Reynolds, so they put prosthetics on my face and I did the stunt. I walked up to Jerry and asked if he remembered me. With all the makeup on he said he didn't. I did the stunt one more time and I was finished. I'd taken off the prosthetics and walked up to Jerry again and asked if he recognized me then. He almost fell off this scaffolding to come down and see me. He gave me this huge hug. That's the kind of guy he is."

Of course the Girl Scouts were hilarious, but Gimple specifically remembers a little round lady, an extra, wearing a gray smock and a black beret. "She really had some moves," Gimple said. "After I am thrown across the bar, my head slams into the jukebox. That's when this round woman in the beret behind her and everyone else starts bobbing to the Bee Gees's "Stayin Alive." All I recall is the extras twitching, getting into the groove, arms shooting up in the air, dancing to the Bee Gees."

Julie Hagerty said they had two wonderful

choreographers for the dance sequence. Lester Wilson, who had choreographed John Travolta in *Saturday Night Fever* and a great choreographer, a guy named Mahoney who did a lot of work at the Walt Disney Studio. Hagerty said she and Hays rehearsed quite a bit at Disney for a few weeks for the disco scene at the 'seediest dive on the wharf.' It was worse than Detroit. The Magumba bar was populated with 'every reject and cutthroat from Bombay to Calcutta. Neither Hagerty nor Hays were real dancers. In the scene Striker approaches Elaine. In rehearsal they moved away from the camera to the left, that's how they learned the move. It was Hays who suggested he approach Hagerty like a wild animal and they began to circle each other, like lions in a jungle.

Stephen Stucker

a.k.a. Johnny Henshaw-Jacobs

"Oh, it's a big pretty white plane with red stripes, curtains in the windows and wheels and it looks like a big Tylenol."

Stephen Stucker knew how to steal a scene. His character Johnny pulled the plug on the runway lights, wanted to make a brooch out of newspapers and never wanted coffee. "I really appreciated Stephen Stucker," said Nielsen Disney of the late actor. "I think he was my favorite character. He'd just show up as blips throughout the movie, just popping through.

Strucker had an immense stage presence, knew how to work an audience both live and on film. His animated face would gently pull you into his world. "He prances. He pirouettes. He bats his eyelashes. He growls. He sings out facts about Barbara Stanwyck from his desk," Hagerty said. "He takes over press conferences and rolls his eyes and tickles serious men/"

"Stephen Stucker wrote his own stuff for the movie, that's how much we trusted him," David Zucker said. "At the Kentucky Fried Theater, he used to do this bit, "Me John Big Tree," then he'd put his arms out like he was a big tree, and then he'd get down on his knees and put his ear to the ground and say, "Wagon train comes three, maybe four day away," like how the Native Americans in the old Westerns used to put their ear to the ground to hear what was coming. We shot that but cut it from the film and we still wish it had stayed."

Can you steal a movie with just some quotes? Here are a few quotes from Johnny Henshaw-Jacobs in the movie.

Johnny, what can you make out of this? "*"This? Why, I can make a hat or a brooch or a pterodactyl."*

Bad news. The fog is getting thicker. *"And Leon is getting laaaarrrrger."*

What kind of plane is it? *"Oh, it's a big, white, pretty plane with red stripes, curtains in the windows and wheels and it looks like a big Tylenol."*

Mayday! Mayday! What the heck is that? *"Why, that's the Russian New Year. We can have a parade and serve hot hors d'oeuvres.*

(Stucker is wrapped in phone cords in the tower.) "Auntie Em, Uncle Henry, Toto! It's a twister, It's a twister!

Johnny, how 'bout some more coffee? *"No, thanks!"*

Criticizing the wardrobe of the Captain's wife. *"Where did you get that dress, it's awful. And those shoes and that coat, jeeeeez!"*

I need the best man on this. Someone who knows that plane inside and out and won't crack under pressure. *"How about Mr. Rogers?"*

Now your husband and the others are alive, but unconscious. *"Just like Gerald Ford."*

Even diehard fans of *Airplane!* may not realize David Letterman read for Ted Striker and the Zucker's thought he was really funny. (You can find his audition online, and he really wasn't that funny.) This was early in his "Late Show" career. "I think maybe his agents pushed him to come in or something, because he really didn't want to," David Zucker said. "It's funny, because Letterman's a satirist and a comic, and he doesn't take himself seriously enough, in a way, to be an actor. Even so, he actually came in to read for *Airplane!*"

Letterman read the scene where Ted Striker is in the hospital painting, lamenting his piloting skills. He was actually in the bed. Letterman is a guy who's brilliant at being a talk show and a stand-up. In fact, we went and watched him do stand-up before he came in, when he was at the Comedy Store in Los Angeles, and he was so good, especially when this one heckler started to get on him. "He was so good as a comic," David Zucker said. "You almost couldn't laugh. He was jaw-dropping in his act. So he clearly was—and is—a brilliant guy. He's also *clearly* not an actor."

Shooting The Film

No wonder you're upset. She's lovely. And a darling figure... supple, pouting breasts... firm thighs. It's a shame you two don't get along

A lot of the film was shot in Culver City and they had two soundstages there, so they weren't on the Paramount lot. It was a little soundstage. Koch really believed in ZAZ and their movie. It was his baby and he took it under his wing and cared for it. It was very low budget and Koch had to keep everything moving, functioning. Koch was like a guardian.

ZAZ began filming at the Culver City Studios, just east of MGM, where they had filmed the exterior of the main building for use as Tara, the magnificent plantation home in *Gone With The Wind*.

Leslie Nielsen whipped out his little 'wind' machine constantly on the set of *'Airplane!* "I felt like I'd made it," Hays said. "The first day I arrived at the studio gate, gave the guard my name, and drove onto the lot in my 1966 Ford Mustang convertible," Hays said. "I know it was mine as they'd painted *Robert Hays* right on the sign. I parked and then went in search of my dressing room, or closet, whatever they had for me. I would have been happy with either."

Like in the military, in the film business you hurry up and wait. As an actor you've got to get there early and you're only called when they're ready for you. "I don't know how many times I worked on films or television shows where I had a 6:00 a.m. call and they wouldn't get to me until 4:00 in the afternoon," Hays said. "When you work on location outside of the radius of L.A. (75 miles, I think) they put you up in a hotel or motel, but when we're working in Los Angeles, you stay at home. That means when you have a 6 a.m call, you're up at 4 or 5 a.m., drive to the set, go through makeup, grab an egg burrito and be ready on the set by 6:30. Let me tell you, those burritos were dangerous. Hard to stop at just one. People have a tendency to put on weight when they're filming, especially with a good caterer."

ZAZ shot a good chunk of the film at LAX as Ted Striker exits his cab, which he left on the curb, makes his way through the terminal while karate chopping, punching and disengaging himself from a barrage of religious zealots.

When Striker brings in the plane for a final landing, fans will remember him sweating profusely. Some might be more inclined to think of it like you would Niagara Falls flowing over his his skull and down his face. If you're wondering how special effects pulled that off--you'd have to be familiar with something called a Hudson Sprayer. It resembles an old-time fire extinguisher. Farmers often use them to spray for weeds or whatever. It has a ring handle around the top like a fire extinguisher, with a handle in the center of the ring that you pump up and down to pressurize the tank. There's a thin hose that comes out of the bottom. They attached an extension hose to it so it could run up under Hay's shirt to the back of his head. There it was attached to a 'halo' of tubing that fit around his head. When they turned the valve, the air would force the water into the hose and up into the halo. They poked a bunch of holes in that part of the halo over Hay's forehead and then combed his hair over it to hide it. It came out as a trickle at first, but gradually they opened the valve up, more and more, until the aforementioned Niagara Falls was in full bloom. Hay's recalled they did several takes. Each time he was obviously soaking wet. After going to wardrobe and makeup and hair where they would change his shirts, fix his hair and dry him off.

There was more fun with water ahead. In *From Here to Eternity*, which ZAZ claim they never saw, there was a kiss that lasted what felt like several days between Burt Lancaster and Deborah Kerr. The special effects crew set up a portable water tank made of canvas and used a gas powered portable water pump to fill the tank with 10,000 gallons of icy cold water from the ocean. When they released the water to simulate the waves washing over Ted and Elaine, the water pressure rushing over them was so intense it rolled their eyelids back and burned them with salt and sand. Quite uncomfortable.

Hagerty said it's something she'll never forget. "Robert could see the water coming but I couldn't. He just held me and said 'just hang on, I've got you.' That's the kind of guy he is, always making you feel safe and comfortable. In that scene, I'll never forget the catfish that ended up in my hair. It was alive and I could feel it writhing above my head," Hagerty explained. The early scenes in the airport at LAX gave you an immediate idea of what to expect in the movie. We see Striker approach the terminal, walking briskly. He came home earlier that night to a note from Elaine saying she was leaving him--basically a 'Dear Ted' letter. As he walks through the terminal, he's accosted by groups of every flavor wanting donations--Hare Krishnas, Save the Whales, Save the Planet, and Help Jerry's Kids. One of the zealots, while trying to pin a flower on Striker's leather jacket, was so persistent, Striker sluffs it off, leaving the zealot with the coat. "If you're old enough to remember the 1980s, you'll recall airports were barraged by people asking for donations, most notably the Hare Krishnas," Hagerty said. Shooting at the airport was one of my fondest recollections of the production.

"My main memory of working during the airport scenes was that it was so much fun," Hagerty said. "You always knew when Robert Hays was coming on the set. You'd hear a door open and then some laughter. A few moments later you'd hear a voice coming closer, then more laughter. Bob was cracking everybody up on the set. People just kept laughing. He was so good looking, like Clark Gable or Robert Redford. Robert has always been so generous and kind." Everything shot at LAX had to be done in one day as it was so busy. "The shooting schedule was crammed full and we couldn't tie up the terminal forever. ZAZ would just say, "We gotta go," so there was a lot of pressure on everybody."

The *Airplane!* set was a mockup of a Boeing 707 that was split down the middle so it could be shot from the cockpit looking back down the aisle, from the back looking up toward the cockpit. They could split it apart to shoot the passengers on the right or on the left side. Sections of the cockpit itself were able to be moved so you could shoot looking forward, from either side, or, by removing the nose. They could also shoot looking looking over our shoulders in the pilot and co-pilot seats. It gave ZAZ a lot of options in their shooting, which was great considering that so much of the film took place on the plane.

The African Village scene was shot at the abandoned Los Angeles Zoo at Griffith Park on July 27,

1979. In the script these were scenes 95, 96, 97, even though you never shoot a movie in order and this was the 28th day of shooting. Hays said he remembers the zoo had these huge chunks of concrete, old animal cages and of course the elephant that was standing behind Hagerty during her Tupperware segment of the scene.

"I just played it very straight, like I was talking Tupperware to ladies in Ohio just like them," Hagerty said. "The 'Upcoming monsoon months' segment was just like talking about the weather in Ohio. When we did the scene in the cockpit where I was reinflating Otto, I truthfully didn't get the joke at the time. All I knew was I was blowing up this doll. (You'll remember this is the scene where it looks like Elaine is performing fellatio on her autopilot, Otto.) "I should have known when the crew was spinning Otto's head around, but I didn't. I was just a 24 year-old girl from Ohio."

"The shoot on that day was close enough to home where we drove ourselves," Hays said. "I remember parking next to Julie near the old entrance to the zoo. We got to our trailers, which were not too fancy. In reality, it was one trailer with four compartments used as a dressing area. They did have our names on them so I suppose that' something. They also had a couch, bathroom and sitting area. We shot for a couple days at the zoo and if you needed a break or weren't required to be on set you could take a snooze on your couch. On our way in, we'd stop by the food truck. It's like a food vendor you see at a street corner or event with the side window that slides open, kind of a chuck wagon. Sometimes an assistant would take a food order when actors were in hair and makeup and bring it back to them. At lunch and dinner they served a more formal meal and there are always craft services tables with snacks and drinks."

The African Village sequence was also where Ted Striker developed his 'drinking problem.' "Julie was hilarious in that scene demonstrating her Tupperware," Hays said. "After you slip into costume you get your sides (Scenes to be shot that day.) Normally, you shoot what's on those pages and sometimes there are some changes on the set. Some new pages or deletions. Once you get to the shooting location, you can stuff the sides into your special director chair with your name emblazoned on the back.

It's often a rough week when you're shooting. A lot of people don't realize we get weekends off like everybody else. If you went seven days straight you'd go mad."

Jive Talkin'

"Chump don' want no help, chump don' get da help."

I don't think Barbara Billingsley, was ever able to divorce herself from the jive talking passenger in *Airplane!*--and it turned out to be a blessing for her. Jive is said to be derived from one of two places, depending on who you ask. It's either a slang language mostly used by jazz musicians, or it stemmed from slaves that didn't want their owners to know what they were talking about, a hidden language. When Al White and Norman Gibbs read for ZAZ, they cracked up. There was no question they were going to cast them. In the original script Norman's part read, "Mo fo, shi' man, wha' fo'." It meant absolutely nothing. When White and Gibbs came in, ZAZ said they apologized profusely and explained that that was the best that three Jewish guys from Milwaukee could do. White looked at the script and couldn't make hide nor hair of the actual verbiage, but got a sense of what they wanted. They wanted jive as a language. Gibbs and

White worked on it together. White got a couple of books, one focused on black English by J.L. Dillard, the second book was on black language. They just tried to come up with what they felt was jive. What they ended up saying does mean something. It's not a bunch of gibberish, it did actually mean something.

"The whole notion for jive dialogue originated from when we saw _Shaft_," said Abrahams. "We went and saw it and didn't understand what they were saying. So we did our best to write jive talk for the script." During the audition, Norman Alexander Gibbs and Al White, old high school friends, delivered a spot on exchange in jive. They were immediately cast as First Jive Dude and Second Jive Dude respectively.

"We came up with the individual dialogue in the movie," said White. "They wanted jive as a language, which it is not. Jive is only a word here or a phrase there. We actually created a language," said Gibbs.

"I was sent the script and I thought it was the craziest script I've ever read," recalled Barbara Billingsley in an interview on CBS. "My part wasn't written, it just said I talked jive. I met the producer and

I said I would do it. I met the two black fellows that taught me jive. It wasn't hard for me to learn." In the movie, 'Jive Dude 1' was trying to convey to Elaine that 'Second Jive Dude' had gotten sick from eating the fish. The stewardess Elaine has no idea what the guys are saying, but scribbled something on her pad. That's when Billingsley comes to her aid, explaining she speaks jive. When ZAZ wrote Billingsley's jive dialogue and instructed her in its proper elocution, she was very intent on getting it right. When she got up and said, "Excuse me, stewardess, I speak jive," she nailed it. But when she said, 'Cut me some slack, Jack,' she had a little trouble with that line. "They explained 'cut me some' is 'cummesome,' Billingsley said. "So they worked on that a little bit, and when I finally got it, we were all so pleased."

Sequel? Fuhgeddaboudit

"The life of everyone on board depends upon just one thing: finding someone back there who can not only fly this plane, but who didn't have fish for dinner."

Why make a sequel out of a classic? Most of the time artists had to beg to make the first movie. The answer is money. Paramount owned *Airplane!* so the sequel was up to them. ZAZ didn't try to talk them out of it. They had the philosophy the studio didn't owe them anything. They had the assets. Like Mo Green in Godfather II, it was just business--only ZAZ didn't get a bullet in the eye. When asked to make the sequel, ZAZ politely declined. They say they still don't know what kind of money they were turning down as it never got to the discussion stage.

Who Cares What They Think?

"Shanna, they bought their tickets, they knew what they were getting into. I say, let 'em crash."

The film was small, under the radar, and David Zucker said that wasn't a bad thing. "Paramount's big picture at that time was *Urban Cowboy*, so they were busy with that, and the first *Star Trek* movie was coming out and so the studios didn't pay much attention to us." The first screening of the film was a disaster. It wasn't easy to get people to come see a movie with Robert Stack and Lloyd Bridges. There was only one guy in the audience who laughed out loud. He didn't care. "We edited off of one guy's reactions," Zucker said. "Usually you want 300 people to learn from. I should have gotten his name. Then we did a bunch of college campus screenings and they were great. There's nothing worse than spending a few years on a project and having it bomb. We have all our egos and self image and worth tied up into a project. From there it was fairly smooth sailing, it became a hit. The film appears to be even more popular now than it was then, which is saying something since it seemed to break almost every box office record in every theater it played in across the country."

There was no way anyone could have foreseen the success of the film, nobody thought that far ahead. It was an essentially untried comedy.. As production went along the cast and crew thought there might be something to this. When it was tested at college campuses and the audiences went wild, all started believing. The studio would have to run dailies over and over for the studio executives, because everyone wanted to see it. Instead of making up excuses, like having to go brush their teeth. They *really* wanted to see it.

When the reviews started to come in, renown critic Roger Ebert gave *Airplane!* three stars and wrote this style of humor went out with Milton Berle, Jerry Lewis, and knock-knock jokes. That's why it was so funny. "Movie comedies these days are so hung up on being contemporary, radical, outspoken, and cynically satirical that they sometimes forget to be funny," Ebert wrote. "And they've lost the nerve to be as corny as

"Airplane!"

Richard Schickel wrote in Time magazine, *"Airplane!* is a splendidly tacky, totally tasteless, completely insignificant flight, a gooney bird of a movie that looks as if it could never get off the ground and then surprises and delights with its free-spirited aerobatics."

The Hollywood Reporter was glowing with praise. "The direction is as wild and woolly as the script, but the team of Abrahams, Zucker and Zucker have a good eye for visual jocularity and they set the sight gags up for maximum effect. The facetiousness has also been kept to a tight 88-minute running time by Patrick Kennedy's rapid-paced editing.

Happy Landings

"Striker, listen, and you listen close: flying a plane is no different than riding a bicycle, just a lot harder to put baseball cards in the spokes."

Well, there you go. This has been a summation from interviews that were conducted for a book with ZAZ. They screwed me over so I did the best I could. Hopefully you learned something, had a chuckle, or confirmed something you already felt. Despite getting hosed, Airplane! Will always be a special movie for me. As I too am from Shorewood, like ZAZ, I'd like to think I 'got' them. I understand the hideously cold and barren place we come from. At the end of the day, everybody thinks they have a book in them. They probably do, only who wants to read it?

A leaflet, on the other hand...

Made in United States
North Haven, CT
06 February 2023